The Home-mixing Of Fertilizers

Charles Embree Thorne

The Home-mixing Of Fertilizers

Charles Embree Thorne

Ohio Agricultural Experiment Station.

BULLETIN 93

WOOSTER, OHIO, APRIL, 1898.

THE HOME-MIXING OF FERTILIZERS.

NORWALK, OHIO:
THE LANING PRINTING COMPANY.
1898.

ORGANIZATION OF THE

OHIO AGRICULTURAL EXPERIMENT STATION.

BOARD OF CONTROL.

The Bulletins of this Station are issued at irregular intervals. They are paged consecutively, and an index is included with the Annual Report, which constitutes the final number of each yearly volume.

BULLETIN

OF THE

Ohio Agricultural Experiment Station

NUMBER 93.   APRIL, 1898.

THE HOME-MIXING OF FERTILIZERS.

BY C. E. THORNE.

THE CHEMISTRY OF FERTILIZERS.

Ten chemical elements are found to be essential to the growth of agricultural plants. These are carbon, oxygen, hydrogen, nitrogen, phosphorus, potassium, calcium, sulphur, magnesium and iron. While these are required in very different proportions, the entire absence of any one of them means death to the plant. To this list chlorine and sodium, the constituents of common salt, are added by some authors.

The inexhaustible reservoir of carbon and oxygen is the atmosphere. From this the plant absorbs through its foliage its supply of carbon, a supply which is only limited by the amount of water and mineral substances at the disposal of the plant, and by its own capacity for growth.

Oxygen and hydrogen in combination form water, and water is the vehicle in which all the mineral food of the plant is carried to its place. Nitrogen constitutes about four-fifths of the atmosphere and is also found in large quantity in practically all soils; but in its free state in the air and in the condition in which it is found in soil it is not available to vegetation. In fact no one of the substances named except oxygen, and that only in part, can serve as food for the higher plants in their elementary form, but all must be first combined with oxygen.

Charcoal is almost pure carbon. In burning it unites chemically with the oxygen of the air, the black solid passing off in an invisible gas—carbonic acid (carbon di-oxide in modern terminology)—and it is this carbonic acid which the plant breathes in through its foliage and converts, through union with the elements of water, into its carbonaceous tissues.

Oxygen constitutes about one-fifth of the atmosphere; combined with hydrogen—the lightest of gases—it forms water.

Nitrogen, as stated, constitutes about four-fifths of the atmosphere, in which it is simply mixed with oxygen; but when these two gases are mixed in certain proportions in the presence of water and then chemically combined (as by electricity) there is formed the powerfully corrosive liquid known as nitric acid. These examples illustrate the vast difference between simple mixture and chemical combination.

Phosphorus, potassium and calcium are never found in nature in the free state, but are always combined with oxygen, giving us phosphoric acid, potash and lime. Even iron is seldom found in the pure state, but usually as an oxide.

Sulphur is found in volcanic regions, but it also must be converted into sulphuric acid, by union with oxygen, before it can serve as plant food.

Phosphorus and potassium are not only combined with oxygen, but these simpler compounds are again recombined in nature. The combination of phosphoric acid and lime, known as phosphate of lime, constitutes the mineral basis of bone, and deposits of fossil bone are found in Carolina, Florida, Tennessee and other parts of the world.

Potash is a permanent constituent of granite rocks, but the chief sources of supply are the ashes of plants and certain mines in Germany where it is found as a crude salt, combined with muriatic and sulphuric acids.

Manures and fertilizers are used for the purpose of conveying to the soil the three elements, nitrogen, phosphorus and potassium in available and convenient form; experience having demonstrated that practically all soils contain an abundant supply of the remaining minerals required for plant growth.

CARRIERS OF NITROGEN.

Liquid nitric acid might be used for fertilizing purposes, but there are other forms in which nitrogen is not only less expensive, but more convenient to store and handle. NITRATE OF SODA, a combination of nitric acid and soda, is found in extensive deposits in Chili, in a region where no rain ever falls, and is mined, refined and shipped to Europe and the United States in large quantity. Chemically pure nitrate of soda contains about 16½ per cent. of nitrogen, 56½ per cent. oxygen and 27 per cent. of sodium. It is usually sold on the basis of 96 per cent. pure sodium nitrate, equivalent to 15.8 per cent. nitrogen. It is a coarse salt, easily soluble in water, and for this reason should not be used in the fall, as it is liable to be dissolved and carried away by the winter rains. When sown on wheat after spring growth has begun it produces a marked effect on the young plants, giving them a dark green color.

It is especially adapted to most spring crops, because of its quick action and complete availability, and is considerably used in the compounding of factory-mixed fertilizers in the eastern states. It is practically never used in such fertilizers in Ohio, because materials showing equal percentages of nitrogen under chemical analysis may be purchased here at far less cost than nitrate of soda. Moreover, as fertilizers are used chiefly on the wheat crop in Ohio, nitrate of soda would be at the same time a more expensive and less suitable source of nitrogen for general use in Ohio than these other materials, which will be described further on, because its easy solubility renders it liable to be washed out of the soil by the winter rains.

Nitric acid, or more strictly nitric oxide, is, as has been stated, a combination of nitrogen and oxygen. Nitrogen forms a compound with the other constituent of water (hydrogen) known as ammonia. Ammonia is a gas consisting chemically of about 82½ per cent. by weight of nitrogen and 17½ per cent. hydrogen. When stable manure is allowed to heat, this gas is produced, through the union of the nitrogen of the manure with the hydrogen of the moisture present, and the pungent odor tells us that the manure is losing the chief part of its value.

Possibly because of the association of ammonia with stable manure it has become customary in the fertilizer trade to estimate the nitrogen of fertilizers altogether on the basis of ammonia, and a standard grade of nitrate of soda, containing 15.8 per cent nitrogen, would be said to contain 19 per cent. ammonia, although it really contains no ammonia whatever.

The fact that this method of calculation tends to magnify the actual contents of the fertilizer sack is probably not without influence in perpetuating the custom.

Ammonia combines with sulphuric acid forming SULPHATE OF AMMONIA. This, like nitrate of soda, is a coarse salt. It is produced in large quantity as a refuse product in the manufacture of illuminating gas, and is sold at prices which bring it within reach of the fertilizer mixer. Pure sulphate of ammonia contains over 21 per cent. nitrogen, and it is usually sold on a guarantee of 25 per cent. ammonia.

When used under similar conditions nitrate of soda and sulphate of ammonia seem to be almost equally effective as carriers of nitrogen to vegetation.

ORGANIC NITROGEN. All living tissues contain more or less nitrogen; it is a conspicuous element of the excreta of animals and men; it is found in many of the waste products of manufactures in which vegetable or animal products constitute the crude materials, and the wastes of the great slaughterhouses and fish packing establishments have within recent years become a most important source of fertilizer nitrogen.

Of these wastes, DRIED BLOOD is one of considerable importance. It is variable in composition, but should contain 12 to 13 per cent. of nitrogen, equivalent to 14 to 16 per cent. of "ammonia" and its nitrogen is found to be quickly available to vegetation.

THE FERTILIZER UNIT: In the fertilizer market it has become customary to quote many fertilizing materials at so much per unit; the unit meaning one per cent., or 20 pounds per ton. The present quotation in the New York market for dried blood, "high grade, western fine ground," is $1.75 to $1.77½ per unit, which would mean $24.50 to $28.50 per ton for blood of the grade above mentioned, the unit being always reckoned on the basis of ammonia. On the same date nitrate of soda was quoted at $1.77½ to $1.80 per unit cash, or just a shade more than the price of dried blood. In fact, in the eastern markets the price of nitrate of soda regulates the price of other AMMONIATES, as nitrogen bearing materials are called, and the price in the eastern markets regulates the price in the west since the consumption of fertilizing materials is far greater in the seaboard states than farther inland.

TANKAGE is a slaughter house refuse largely used in the mixing of fertilizers. In its manufacture the scraps of meat, tendon and bone which have no other value are thrown into tanks in which their grease is extracted, after which the residue is dried and ground. As found in the market it is a fine, dry meal, having but little odor, and serves as a useful carrier of both nitrogen and phosphoric acid. It is variable in composition, running from 6 to 10 per cent of "ammonia" and from 10 to 35 per cent. of "BONE PHOSPHATE," bone phosphate being that compound of phosphoric acid and lime which is found in bones, and which contains about 46 per cent. of phosphoric acid united with about 54 per cent. of lime. A standard grade of tankage is called 9 and 20, meaning that it contains 9 per cent. of "ammonia" and 20 per cent. of "bone phosphate," equivalent to 9 per cent. of phosphoric acid. This grade of tankage was quoted at $15 to $16 per ton in Chicago in March, these quotations being of course for car loads.

Tankage ranges as low as a 6 and 35 or 6 and 40 grade and as high as a 10 and 10 grade, or from a material consisting chiefly of bone to one approaching dried blood in composition. The nitrogen in tankage, especially in the lower grades, is not so quickly available as in blood, but when used in proper combinations tankage appears to be a very useful fertilizing material.

Tankage and fish scrap, a similar refuse from the fish packing houses are, in fact, the basis of practically all the factory-mixed fertilizers made in Ohio, fertilizers of every desired composition being made by mixing tankage, acid phosphate and muriate of potash in different proportions. Many have the idea that a "filler" of some sort is required to complete the fertilizer, but this is a mistake. It is only the low grade fertilizer that needs any filler, and such filler is always an adulteration.

HOOFS, HORNS, HAIR AND WOOL WASTE carry considerable percentages of nitrogen, which is still more slowly available than that of bone and tankage. Hoof meal is becoming a regular article of trade as a source of ammonia in fertilizers; but in a single experiment, made at this station on the wheat crop of 1896-7, hoof meal failed to produce any increase of crop, even when acidulated.

LEATHER shows a considerable percentage of nitrogen in the chemist's laboratory, but it decomposes so slowly in the soil as to be practically worthless for fertilizing purposes.

CARRIERS OF PHOSPHORIC ACID.

The phosphoric acid of ordinary fertilizers is invariably combined with lime. Animal bone contains about 60 per cent. of bone phosphate, a compound having about 46 per cent. of phosphoric acid, combined with 54 per cent. of lime, and the large use of bones as a source of phosphoric acid has led to the general use of the term "bone phosphate" as indicating a combination of phosphoric acid and lime in these proportions. A bone meal, therefore, showing 4 per cent. nitrogen and 23 per cent. phosphoric acid, would be said to carry 5 per cent. "ammonia" and 50 per cent. "bone phosphate."

The principal sources of the phosphoric acid of the fertilizers sold in Ohio, are the animal refuse from slaughter houses, glue factories and fish packing houses, and the deposits of phosphatic rock found in Carolina, Florida and Tennessee. Other sources are the apatite rocks of Canada and the slag resulting from the manufacture of steel from phosphatic ores. At present, the price of fertilizer phosphoric acid is controlled by the cost of production in the southern states.

These phosphatic rocks are ground into a fine meal, to which the name "floats" is given; but in this condition their phosphoric acid is almost completely insoluble in water or weak acids, and is therefore worth but very little as a fertilizer. To make it available it is treated with about an equal weight of sulphuric acid, an operation involving a certain amount of chemical knowledge and technical skill, and performed to best advantage with special machinery and appliances. The treated rock is called "ACID PHOSPHATE."

Bone charcoal is used in large quantities in the refining of sugar. After serving this purpose it is treated with sulphuric acid, making what is termed "dissolved bone black," or "SUPERPHOSPHATE." This material has been considered a standard carrier of phosphoric acid. It should contain about 16 per cent. of available phosphoric acid. In bone black, as in Carolina rock, the phosphoric acid is very slow of action until treated with acid. The term superphosphate is also applied to acid phosphate.

In their description of the various conditions of phosphoric acid in fertilizers chemists use the terms "insoluble," "soluble," "reverted," and "available." "Insoluble" acid is that which will not dissolve in water nor in a standard solution of ammonium citrate. "Soluble" acid dissolves in water. "Reverted" acid has been in solution but has become temporarily insoluble in water, yet it is still soluble in ammonium citrate of a given strength. In this condition it is found that plants make use of it rapidly, and it is therefore termed "reverted" or "available," the latter term being used also to include both soluble and reverted acid.

Dissolved bone black should contain 15 to 17 per cent. of available phosphoric acid and acid phosphates of good quality from 14 to 16 percent. The phosphatic slag from steel manufacture shows 16 to 20 per cent. of phosphoric acid, which seems to be nearly all available, though not responding to the same tests in the laboratory as those employed for the bone and rock phosphates.

In experiments made at this station, which have now extended over 10 years, practically the same increase has been recovered from equal quantities of available phosphoric acid of dissolved bone black and acid phosphate and the total phosphoric acid of slag meal.

CARRIERS OF POTASH.

The chief source of the potash found in Ohio fertilizers is the MURIATE OF POTASH, a coarse salt of which the chief supply of the world is now drawn from mines near Stassfurt, Germany. It is ordinarily sold on the basis of 80 per cent. muriate, which is equivalent to about $50\frac{1}{2}$ per cent actual potash. It usually contains about 15 per cent common salt and small quantities of other impurities.

KAINIT is a potash salt of a lower grade, analyzing usually 12 to 13 per cent. actual potash, which is considerably used in the Eastern states; but the large amount of useless material on which freight must be paid makes it a more expensive source of potash to the Ohio farmer than the muriate, although the latter sells at a much higher price per ton To illustrate: in January kainit was quoted in New York at $9.60 to $10.65 per ton and muriate of potash at $37.00 to $38.00 per ton. At these prices the pound of actual potash would cost in New York about $3\frac{3}{4}$ cents in the muriate and 4 cents in the kainit, but when the freight to Ohio is added the cost of the pound of potash is increased to 6 cents or more in kainit and to only $4\frac{1}{4}$ cents in the muriate.

Unleached hard wood ashes should contain 5 to 6 per cent. of potash and 1 to 2 per cent. of phosphoric acid, averaging 7 per cent. of the two. At \$6.00 per ton or less, freight included, unleached ashes are a reasonably cheap source of potash; but when the price exceeds this sum the cost of the pound of actual potash is greater than in the muriate, although the latter may cost \$42 to \$44 per ton, freight included.

It is true that ashes contain 25 to 40 per cent. of lime, averaging 30 per cent., and when lime is needed some allowance should be made on this account.

Potash constitutes more than half the total ash from corn cobs, a fact which may well be utilized by those who are in reach of elevators where cobs are used largely for fuel. Corn cob ash, if pure, is probably worth nearly as much for fertilizing purposes as muriate of potash, pound for pound.

On most Ohio soils phosphoric acid appears to be the constituent of fertility first exhausted, and because of the marked effect following the use of acid phosphate and its comparatively low price it is often used without any other addition. In the experiments of this Station, however, which have been conducted on various soils, a considerably larger crop has invariably been produced when nitrogen has been added to the phosphoric acid, and in most cases the crop has been still further increased by the addition of potash; but in general the effect of potash has been greater when it has been used in combination with both nitrogen and phosphoric acid.

THE MANUFACTURE OF FERTILIZERS.

The phosphatic rocks of South Carolina, Florida and Tennessee are quarried and dried, and either ground into powder near the point of production or else shipped without grinding. The present quotations for ground rock at Charleston, South Carolina, are \$5.50 to \$5.60 per ton of 2,000 ℔s., and \$3.50 to \$3.60 per ton of 2,000 ℔s., for the same rock dried but unground. It is largely shipped north by ocean freight, and the ground and acidulated rock is now offered in bulk in carload lots in Baltimore at \$7.50 per ton, or at \$8.50 per ton in sacks of 200 ℔s. For larger lots the price is of course still lower.

Some of the larger establishments purchase the unground rock, grind it and treat it with sulphuric acid, in some cases manufacturing the acid for this purpose. The market price for such acid is about the same as that given for acidulated rock, and acid and rock are used in approximately equal quantities, varying somewhat of course according to strength of acid and composition of rock. The Tennessee supply of raw rock of great purity is rapidly developing the manufacture of acid phosphate in Ohio.

The manufacture of the acid and grinding and treating of the rock are operations which can be performed with greatest economy on the large scale, with special equipment, and should not be undertaken on the farm, and the same is true of the manufacture of tankage.

Both acid phosphate and tankage are in the condition of fine, dry powder, ready for use in the fertilizer drill. In fact both are largely used directly as fertilizers without the addition of any other material. Being in this mechanical condition it will be seen that they may be as readily mixed together as, for instance, corn meal and bran, and in consequence of this facility of mixing countless so-called "manufacturers" of fertilizers are to be found throughout the country who are simply mixers and nothing more.   A few large establishments do all the manufacturing, and from these the mixers purchase their materials which they stir together in various proportions, and put upon the market as special fertilizers for corn, wheat, tobacco, potatoes, fruit, etc.

To the mixture of tankage and acid phosphate potash is occasionally added, usually in the form of the muriate, as that is both a cheap and an effective carrier of potash.   It is a coarse, dry salt, which may be readily mixed with the acid phosphate and tankage.

THE OBJECT OF ACIDULATION.

It has been stated above that the treatment of the rock phosphates with sulphuric acid is necessary to make their phosphoric acid readily available. The effect of this treatment is to make the phosphoric acid soluble in water, and although a portion of it soon becomes temporarily insoluble again it does not return to its former condition but remains in a form in which it may be dissolved by weak acids.

Raw bone meal is practically insoluble in its ordinary condition, but when incorporated with the soil the animal matter which it contains decays and thus brings the phosphoric acid into solution ; but when this animal matter is burnt out, as in making charcoal, the bone phosphate becomes as insoluble as the rock phosphate, and needs similar treatment to make its phosphoric acid available.   This treatment makes what is called a "superphosphate" or "dissolved bone phosphate," both terms being applied alike to the material, whether the original source be bone or rock.

In fact, there is a considerable prejudice against the rock phosphates, and the fertilizer mixers are generally careful to describe their materials as "bone phosphates."   For instance, the acid phosphate which has been used regularly in the Station's experiments for years, is labeled on the sack "———'s Dissolved Soluble Bone Phosphate."   Our orders have called simply for "acid phosphate," and the material is acid phosphate, containing no animal bone whatever.

It is evident that the smaller the particles to which the bone or rock is reduced by grinding the more readily they may be attacked by solvents or by soil ferments, and in this respect there has been a great improvement in recent years.   The reports of the Secretary of the Ohio State Board of Agriculture show that less than 42 per cent. of the "bone and untreated organic matter," analyzed under the direction of that office in 1882, was classed as "fine," whereas nearly 75 per cent. was so classed in 1897.

In the experiments of this Station two plots, Nos. 26 and 27, lying side by side, are receiving fertilizers calculated to carry equal quantities of nitrogen, phosphoric acid and potash, the phosphoric acid being given in the form of raw bone meal to Plot 26 and in that of acid phosphate to Plot 27, the nitrogen being given in dried blood and nitrate of soda equally to both plots, except that allowance is made for the nitrogen carried by the bone, and the potash being given as muriate equally to both plots.   This test is being made in four separate series of experiments, two on the central farm at Wooster and two at the Northeastern sub-station at Strongsville, Cuyahoga county, the test being made on each farm in a five crop rotation of corn, oats, wheat, clover and timothy and in a three crop rotation of potatoes, wheat and clover, the fertilizers being applied to the grain and potato crops and the hay crops following without further application.

Up to the present date 9 crops of wheat, 6 of oats, 8 of corn, 5 of potatoes and 9 of hay have been harvested in this test, 37 crops in all, giving the following total increase per acre:

	Plot 26.	Plot 27.
Wheat, bushels of grain	77.66	74.62
Oats, bushels of grain	71.66	70.17
Corn, bushels of grain	28.54	43.20
Potatoes, bushels	81.14	127.78
Straw and stover, lbs	13,731	12,826
Hay, lbs	5,804	3,542

It will be observed that the wheat and especially the hay crops show a decided superiority for Plot 26, while the corn and potato crops give better yields on Plot 27, thus supporting the inference that when quick action is the chief consideration, then a superphosphate should be used; but that for crops of longer season, such as wheat and hay, and especially wheat followed by hay, the total effect from finely ground bone may be fully equal to that from superphosphate.

THE ACIDULATION OF TANKAGE.

The claim has been made for certain fertilizer manufacturers that they treat with sulphuric acid the tankage as well as the Carolina rock, which they use in their work, and it is insisted that the object of such treatment is not only to make the phosphoric acid more soluble but also to " 'fix' the ammonia, and make it available to crops but not liable to wasteful decay in or on the soil."

In other words, the same treatment which liberates the phosphoric acid of the tankage "fixes" its ammonia!

In point of fact, the treatment of ordinary tankage with sulphuric acid has been almost if not altogether abandoned of recent years. It has been learned that fine grinding is of much greater importance, in the treatment of animal matter, than acidulation, since such grinding facilitates the action of the ferment organisms of the air and soil which are the active agents in producing decomposition.

When fresh horse manure is thrown into a heap it very soon "heats," decomposition sets in rapidly and ammonia is liberated, escaping into the atmosphere as a gas. The surest way to prevent this loss is to spread the manure in a thin layer over the soil, and if it can be lightly covered with loose earth, so much the better.

Tankage, or similar matter, if moistened and exposed in heaps to a warm atmosphere would also heat, and ammonia would be evolved; but in the very thin layers in which it is applied as a fertilizer its decay will be relatively slow, and any ammonia liberated will be held by the soil or caught by the roots of the growing plants.

In fact, if there were any occasion for treating the nitrogen of tankage it would be to make it decompose more rapidly, and not to prevent any "wasteful decomposition."

Those who have used tankage alone as a fertilizer have sometimes been disappointed in the result, because the material has become available so slowly that the crop to which it was applied got little benefit; but in ordinary, factory-mixed fertilizers tankage is mixed with acid phosphate, and the quickly soluble phosphoric acid of the acid phosphate starts the young plants into vigorous growth and enables them to make use, later on, of the less active materials in the tankage.

In the experiments of this Station the effect of phosphoric acid seems to be especially marked in the early life of the plant. The plots of wheat in the fall or of corn or oats in the spring which show the first effect of the fertilizer are those and those only which have received phosphoric acid. The plots which have received potash or nitrogen without phosphoric acid cannot be distinguished from the unfertilized plots until later in the season; hence the importance of an early supply of available phosphoric acid to start the young plants and give them vigor to begin foraging for themselves at the earliest date possible. If, to plants thus started, a continuous supply of fertility be offered in materials becoming available throughout the season, the best conditions for maximum crops will have been given, so far as supply of soil food is concerned.

This condition seems to apply to practically all the soils of Ohio upon which artificial fertilizers are being used.

The wholesale price per ton of sulphuric acid, of the grade required for the acidulation of fertilizers, is about half that of tankage and about one-third to one-fourth that at which factory mixed fertilizers are sold to the farmer. The sulphuric acid is not itself a necessary constituent of the fertilizer, and its addition reduces the proportions of those constituents which are needed by the plant; it follows, therefore, that the use of any unnecessary quantity of sulphuric acid must be looked upon as an adulteration, rather than an improvement.

THE FERTILIZER TRADE.

The trade in commercial fertilizers in Ohio was comparatively small twenty years ago. In 1881 the State inspection law was passed, and in 1882 the Secretary of the State Board of Agriculture reported the analysis of 78 brands of fertilizers, with an expenditure by farmers of $495,000 for fertilizers applied to the wheat crop of that year. In 1897 the number of brands analyzed had increased to more than 400, and the expenditure for 1895 was reported by the township assessors at $1,529,000 a sum which is believed by those best informed to be far below the actual cost of fertilizers now used in the state.

The 78 brands of 1882 were furnished by 34 different manufacturers, while 115 firms were represented by the 400 brands of 1897. These figures seem to indicate both that farmers have believed their crops to be profitably increased by the use of fertilizers and that the supplying of the demand for fertilizers has been a remunerative industry; and the latter indication is supported by a comparison of the market quotations on the manufactured products which are used in the compounding of special brands of fertilizers and the prices at which these fertilizers are sold to the farmer. Naturally those who are engaged in a profitable business object to having their profits curtailed by additional competition. The fertilizer trade is no exception to this general rule, and farmers are persuaded that the compounding of fertilizers is an intricate and difficult operation, requiring extensive acquaintance with chemistry, costly machinery, and great technical skill.

The case well illustrates the old adage, that a half truth is a whole falsehood. The production and manufacture of fertilizing materials— that is, the selection, quarrying, grinding and acidulation of phosphatic rock; the drying and grinding of slaughterhouse refuse, the production and refining of such materials as nitrate of soda, sulphate of ammonia and muriate of potash—all these are distinctly manufacturing processes which require chemical or technical knowledge, skill in manipulation and expensive machinery. But these operations are entirely separate and distinct from the compounding of mixed fertilizers. Each of the materials named comes from the manufacturer in condition to be used by itself as a fertilizer and each one is so used for special purposes. The compounding of these materials under a proprietary brand into a mixed fertilizer is no more a manufacture than is the mixing of a ration of corn meal and bran to be fed to a cow. The only difference is that the ration which is designed to be distributed uniformly to thousands or millions of plants requires to be more carefully mixed than that fed to a single cow. If we were feeding each plant by itself, no mixing would be necessary, or if we were giving the different elements of a ration at different times; as for instance, when we apply superphosphate and muriate of potash to wheat in the fall and follow with nitrate of soda in the spring.

This point, of the essential difference between those operations which are legitimately called manufacturing and those which are simply mixing, should be clearly understood.

When the farmer learns that he can mix his own fertilizers and thereby materially reduce their cost, the use of fertilizing materials will be largely increased, and the final outcome will be a benefit and not an injury to the legitimate trade in fertilizers.

DOES HOME-MIXING SAVE ONLY THE COST OF MIXING?

Acting under the advice of this Station a company of farmers bought several carloads of fertilizing materials and mixed for themselves last fall. These farmers first obtained propositions to furnish the desired materials from a considerable number of manufacturers and dealers; selecting those which offered the best terms they concluded their purchase, the materials being guaranteed to carry a definite percentage of the required fertilizing elements. The materials, when received, were mixed according to formulæ furnished by the Station and the result of their use, as shown in the fall growth of the wheat to which they were applied, a few samples of factory mixed fertilizers of similar composition being used alongside, has been such as to lead to much larger purchases for this season's operations. The final cost of their lot of fertilizer, including cost of materials, freight and mixing, was less, by more than five hundred dollars, than the lowest price at which the company was offered an equal quantity of factory-mixed fertilizers of equivalent composition and on the same terms of payment; hence it cannot be said that the only item saved was the bare cost of mixing.

The fact is that the cost of mixing is a very small item among those which go to make up the difference between the cost of materials and the price at which a factory-mixed fertilizer can be sold under the present methods of business. The trade in these fertilizers is built upon a system which involves large expenditures for the salaries and traveling expenses of general agents; for commissions to local dealers; for interest on credit sales, which probably comprise the greater proportion of all sales made at present, and which lead to heavy losses from bad debts, and it is no doubt true that no large margin of profits is left to any one of the several hands through which the ton of factory-mixed fertilizers must pass before it reaches the farmer.

All these items must be provided for in fixing the price of the fertilizer; especially must the interests of the general and local agents be looked after, and therefore the price of the fertilizer in the branded sack cannot be reduced below a point which covers these interests; but in buying the fertilizing materials at first hands all these intermediate expenses are avoided. Both tankage and acid phosphate may be brought direct from original manufacturers, whose business stands on the basis of direct sales to cash buyers.

SOME OBJECTIONS TO HOME-MIXING.

It is claimed that the special machinery employed in the large scale mixing of fertilizers produces a more perfect mixture than can be made with so simple an outfit as a shovel on a barn floor, and this is probably true. It is also true that however thoroughly these materials are mixed together, when they are transported long distances after mixing the finer and heavier particles will settle to the bottom, and by the time the fertilizer sack has reached the field its contents are likely to be in a not more perfect state of mixture than when mixed in the farmer's barn. There are those who claim that the highest perfection in mixing is only attained by what is called "wet mixing," a process in which the materials are treated with acid and allowed to lie for some time before the final grinding and sacking. Aside from the fact that very few, if any manufacturers are now using this method, it must be remembered that when the material becomes dry enough to use in the fertilizer drill it will be dry enough to separate in transportation, and the finer and heavier rock will tend to settle and the coarser and lighter tankage to rise. The farmer, therefore, need have no fear that he cannot mix his materials quite sufficiently for practical purposes if the work be done with reasonable thoroughness.

On this point, however, the testimony of actual experience is better than any theory. The experiment stations of Connecticut, New Jersey and Rhode Island have for years been pointing out to the farmers of their states the possible saving by home-mixing, and those who have followed their advice report a great reduction in cost of fertilizers with equal results in the crop, while the New Jersey Station has made special examination of a large number of such mixtures and found their mechanical condition in every respect equal to that of the best brands of factory-mixed fertilizers on the market.*

Another objection brought against home-mixing is its cost, which has been greatly magnified. On this point we have the testimony of the company of Ohio farmers already referred to, who mixed six carloads for themselves last August, and who state that one man can mix three tons per day. The Rhode Island Experiment Station, in its Bulletin No. 34, illustrates a home-made mixing machine, similar to a large revolving churn, with which fertilizers of all kinds had been mixed for four years in perfect freedom from dust and at a cost of only 50 cents per ton.

It should be distinctly understood, however, that there are but two objects to be attained in the mixing of fertilizers. One is to get particles

*New Jersey Agrl. Expt. Station, Bulletin 113.

of each kind of plant food offered within reach of the roots of every plant, and the other is to save labor in the application.   As already stated, in the experiments at the Station superphosphate and muriate of potash are applied in the fall (being sown with the fertilizer drill) and nitrate of soda is added in the spring, being sown broadcast about the middle of April. Yet the nitrogen thus separately applied has produced a greater increase of crop than any obtained from nitrogen bearing materials mixed with the superphosphate and potash and applied in the fall*.   What the plant wants is an abundant supply of all kinds of food.   It will do the mixing for itself, if its roots have access to such supply.

There is no evidence that any chemical combination takes place outside the plant between the different kinds of food given in the artificial supply.   That is, the phosphoric acid, the potash and the nitrogen do not unite with each other in the soil.   It is only under the influence of the living organism that they are brought into close association with each other.   This point is further illustrated by the fact that the plant takes in its carbon altogether through the foliage, and the mineral constituents of its growth altogether through its roots.   The combination is made within its tissues, carbon being carried from leaf to tip of farthest root, and minerals from root to extremity of topmost leaf, combination taking place at every point between these extremes.

From all this it follows that the most thorough method of applying fertilizers would be to apply each constituent separately, and as the wheat drill is a very effective tillage implement this might be done with perhaps even less expense than to mix them beforehand.

The muriate of potash is usually used in very small quantity, if at all. A fertilizer carrying 2 per cent. of potash and used at the rate of 200 pounds to the acre would be equivalent to a dressing of 4 pounds of actual potash, which would be carried in 8 pounds of the muriate or 80 pounds of unleached hard wood ashes, or in 8 to 10 pounds of pure corn cob ashes.   The muriate of potash closely resembles common salt and may be easily and rapidly sown broadcast, the only difficulty being to sow a small enough quantity, when it is sown alone.   (It is quite possible, however, that potash might be applied in larger quantity and at longer intervals, say once in 8 or 10 years, with equally good results).

Then the fertilizer drill, following with either the tankage or acid phosphate, would take the place of a harrowing, while finally the drill again, crossing the last working, might sow both the wheat and the third constituent of the fertilizer.   It is not necessary that seed and fertilizer should be sown in the same drill row.   On the contrary, experiments made by Prof. A. D. Selby at this Station, and reported in Bulletin 71, (p. 183) have shown that fertilizers have a retarding effect upon germination when placed in immediate proximity to the seed.

AN EXPERIMENT WITH HOME-MIXED FERTILIZERS.

In order to settle definitely some of the points alluded to above this Station began a year ago an experiment in the comparison of a few standard brands of factory-mixed fertilizers with home mixtures, made from tankage, acid phosphate and muriate of potash, in such manner as to du-

*At the Rothamsted Experiment Station it has been found that mangels give a much larger return from nitrate of soda when it is applied, not when the beets are planted, but several weeks later.   See Jour. Roy. Ag. Soc. No. 32 p. 602.

plicate, as nearly as possible, the percentage composition in "ammonia," available and total phosphoric acid, and potash claimed for the proprietary brands.

To this end, four sacks of fertilizers, of 200 pounds each, were ordered in the name of the Station from four of the oldest fertilizer manufacturing establishments in the state; one sack of tankage was similarly ordered of a long established and large manufactory of this article in Ohio; a sack of acid phosphate was ordered from Baltimore and one of muriate of potash from New York.

The four proprietary fertilizers will be called in this report Brands A, B, C, and D. Their minimum analysis, as claimed on the sack, and their actual composition, as given in the official report for 1896 of the Secretary of the Ohio State Board of Agriculture, and as analyzed in the Station laboratory by A. D. Selby and L. M. Bloomfield, are given in Table I, together with that of the tankage and acid phosphate used in our mixtures.

TABLE I.—ANALYSIS OF FERTILIZERS.

Percentage Composition.

Fertilizer.		Ammonia.	Phosphoric acid.			Potash.
			Available.	Insoluble.	Total.	
Brand A............	Claimed ...	4.	8.	2.	10.	4.
	Official	3.90	8.95	....	11.89	4.18
	O. A. E. S.	3.74	10.27	4.72	14.99	3.76
Brand B............	Claimed ...	2.	10.	1.	11.	1.
	Official	0.85	12.41	3.64	16.05	0.66
	O. A. E. S.	1.87	11.06	1.19	12.25	1.81
Brand C............	Claimed ...	2.	8.	2.	10.	1.
	Official......	2.40	5.81	5.38	11.19	1.14
	O. A. E. S.	2.72	10.37	4.21	14.58	2.12
Brand D...........	Claimed ...	1.	6.	1.	7.	1.
	Official......	1.15	5.89	0.83	6.72	1.31
	O. A. E. S.	1.27	6.65	1.28	7.93	1.39
Tankage............	Claimed ...	7.80	....	....	13.49	....
	Official......	8.20	8.32	5.94	14.26	....
	O. A. E. S.	6.30	11.06	6.88	17.88	....
Acid phosphate..	Claimed ...	....	14.	2.	16.	....
	Official* ...	....	14.72	2.23	16.95	....
	O. A. E. S.	....	15.47	1.66	17.13	....

*1897.

It will be observed that there is a considerable divergence between the claimed composition of several of these fertilizers and that found by the chemists, and that the findings in the Station laboratory do not always agree with the official analysis. It should not be assumed that these discrepancies are due to errors in analysis, for the analyses were made by men thoroughly qualified and the discrepancies are far beyond the allowable limits of error in such work.* Our analyses, as a rule, show less va-

---

*One fifth of one per cent. of variation between analyses is regarded as a large margin.

riation from the claimed analysis than do the official analyses.   Our analyses were made on samples sent direct from the factory, while the official analyses were made, (as they should be) on samples selected at random over the State, and these no doubt sometimes had suffered separation in the manner above suggested.

It will be noted that in most cases our analyses show the fertilizer to be well above the guarantee in composition, the margin in several cases being quite large.

It was necessary to begin the experiment before our analyses could be completed, and therefore, taking the claimed composition of the different fertilizers and fertilizing materials as a guide, each brand of the factory mixed fertilizers was duplicated by a mixture of tankage, acid phosphate and muriate of potash, made in the proportions indicated in Table II.   For example, Brand A claims a minimum composition of 4 per cent. ammonia, 10 per cent. in total of phosphoric acid, of which 8 per cent. is available, and 4 per cent of potash.   These minimum percentages therefore mean that each ton of this fertilizer contains not less than 80 pounds of ammonia, 200 pounds of phosphoric acid of which 160 pounds is available, and 80 pounds of potash; and so on for the other brands.

For the tankage used for duplicating these fertilizers is claimed a minimum of 7.8 per cent. of ammonia and 13.49 per cent of phosphoric acid.   The official analysis gives it 8.2 per cent. ammonia and 14.26 per cent. phosphoric acid, of which 8.32 per cent. is available.   For convenience we rated it as containing 8 per cent. ammonia and 14 per cent. phosphoric acid, of which 8 per cent. is available, this rating being higher than the claimed analysis.*

One thousand pounds of such tankage, therefore, would give the 80 pounds of ammonia necessary to duplicate that in Brand A. and 80 pounds of the available phosphoric acid, together with 60 pounds of insoluble acid.   Seven hundred pounds of acid phosphate, of the composition claimed, would give 98 pounds of available phosphoric acid and 14 pounds insoluble acid, making a total of 178 pounds available and 74 pounds insoluble acid, and 160 pounds of muriate of potash would give the 80 pounds of potash required, making a total of 1,860 pounds of these fertilizing materials required to produce a mixture carrying as much ammonia, phosphoric acid and potash as would equal the minimum claims for the factory-mixed fertilizer.   In fact it will be seen by referring to Table III, that the home mixture shows considerably more phosphoric acid than the minimum claim for the proprietary brand, but not more than our analysis shows that brand to have actually contained.   In the same manner each of the other brands was duplicated.

The manufacturers of Brand A charged the Station $3.00 cash for a 200 pound sack, or at the rate of $30.00 per ton, and so on through the list, the Station paying the freight in each case.   The bill rendered for the 200 pound sack of tankage was $1.70 in Cleveland, O., and the freight was 10 cents per hundred pounds, making the total cost at the Station 95 cents per hundred pounds, or $19.00 per ton.   The acid phosphate cost $1.00 per sack, or $10.00 per ton in Baltimore, Md., with 23 cents per hundred pounds for freight, making the total cost per ton at the rate of $14.60. The muriate of potash cost 2 cents per pound in New York and the freight was 27 cents per hundred, bringing the cost up to $2.27 per hundred pounds.

*As it turned out, this tankage was found to contain considerably less ammonia and considerably more phosphoric acid than claimed or shown by the official analysis.

TABLE II.—FORMULÆ BY WHICH PROPRIETARY BRANDS WERE DUPLICATED.

Fertilizer.	Quantity required for ton.	Cost per ton.	Pounds of constituents per ton.				
			Ammonia	Phosphoric acid.			Potash.
				Available.	Insoluble.	Total.	
	Lbs.		Lbs.	Lbs.	Lbs.	Lbs.	Lbs.
Brand A.—Original.........	2,000	$30 00	80	160	40	200	80
Duplicate: Tankage.........	1,000	....	80	80	60	140	....
Acid phosphate	700	....	....	98	14	112	....
Muriate potash.	160	....	....	....	....	....	80
Total	1,860	$18 24	80	178	74	252	80
Brand B.—Original.........	2,000	$25 00	40	200	20	220	20
Duplicate: Tankage.........	500	....	40	40	30	70	....
Acid phosphate	1,450	....	....	203	29	232	....
Muriate potash.	50	....	....	....	....	....	25
Total	2,000	$16 47	40	243	59	302	25
Brand C.—Original.........	2,000	$20 00	40	160	40	200	20
Duplicate: Tankage.........	600	....	48	48	36	84	....
Acid phosphate	900	....	....	126	18	144	....
Muriate potash	50	....	....	....	....	....	25
Total	1,550	$13 41	48	174	54	228	25
Brand D.—Original.........	2,000	$17 50	20	120	20	140	20
Duplicate: Tankage.........	300	....	24	24	18	42	....
Acid phosphate	700	....	....	98	14	112	....
Muriate potash..	50	....	....	....	....	....	25
Total	1,050	$9 10	24	122	32	154	25

In Table III is given the actual composition of the fertilizers and their duplicates, as calculated from the analyses made in our laboratory.

TABLE III—ACTUAL COMPOSITION OF FERTILIZERS AND DUPLICATES.

Fertilizers.	Pounds of constituents per ton.				
	Ammo-nia.	Phosphoric acid.			Potash.
		Available	Insoluble	Total.	
Brand A—Original	75	205	94	299	75
Duplicate	63	218	81	299	75
Brand B—Original	37	221	24	245	36
Duplicate	31	279	58	337	25
Brand C—Original	54	207	84	291	42
Duplicate	38	205	56	261	25
Brand D—Original	25	133	25	158	28
Duplicate	19	141	33	174	25

To duplicate these four brands at these prices cost $18.24 in the case of Brand A; $16.47 for Brand B; $13.41 for Brand C and 9.10 for Brand D, the freight being included in the case of each of the home mixtures, but not in that of the factory brands. The average freight would be not less than $2.00 per ton, which would fully offset the cost of mixing. It will be observed that, if the duplicates shall prove as effective as the original brands, there will be a saving of $11.76 per ton in the case of Brand A, $8.53 in that of Brand B, $6.59 in that of Brand C and $8.40 in that of Brand D, or an average of $8.82 in the four brands .

DIAGRAM SHOWING ARRANGEMENT OF PLOTS IN COMPARISON OF FACTORY-MIXED WITH HOME-MIXED FERTILIZERS.

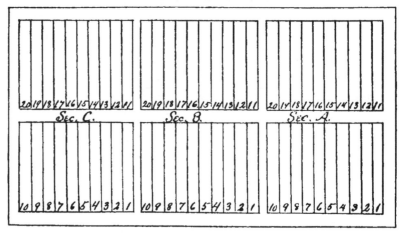

Attention is again called to the fact that these fertilizers and fertilizing materials were all bought on the same basis. The goods were ordered in single sack lots of the original manufacturers, who knew exactly with whom they were dealing, and the prices paid were presumably the regular, cash prices for the goods ordered. In the case of the tankage, acid phosphate and muriate of potash, the prices paid were the publicly quoted retail prices of those materials.

The experiment was located at the North Eastern sub-station, the soil of which is the heavy, white clay of that region, and the work was executed by Mr. Edward Mohn, superintendent. A tract of apparently uniform land was selected and divided into 3 sections of 20 plots each, as per the accompanying diagram, the plots containing one-twentieth acre each, and a rotation was planned to include the three crops, corn, wheat and clover, to follow each other in a three-year course. To start the rotation Sections A and B were planted in corn, and Section C was sown in soy beans, in order to have a leguminous crop preceding the corn crop of the second year. Sections A and B were both fertilized according to plan, thus giving a duplicate test the first year. This proved to be the more important, as Section A was found to be in much poorer condition than Section B, the latter section having grown clover the previous season.

The season proved an unfavorable one for corn, owing to lack of rain, and the crop on Section A especially was very light. The results of the test are given in Table IV. From this table it will be seen that in the general average the home mixtures gave quite as large an increase as did the factory-mixed fertilizers.

TABLE IV—YIELD AND INCREASE OF CROP PER ACRE.

Plot number	Fertilizers	Yield per acre				Increase or decrease (—) per acre					
		Sec. A		Sec. B		Sec. A		Sec. B		Average	
		Grain. Bus.	Stover. Lbs.	Grain. Bus.	Stover. Lbs.	Grain. Bus.	Stover. Lbs.	Grain. Bus.	Stover. Lbs.	Grain. Bus.	Stover. Lbs.
1	None	15.43	1,280	31.29	1,680						
2	Brand A	17.29	1,240	40.71	2,040	3.34	27	8.80	280	6.07	203
3	Duplicate A	17.29	1,320	40.57	2,000	4.81	173	8.05	347	6.43	260
4	None	11.00	1,080	33.14	1,640						
5	Brand B	20.29	1,360	35.00	1,680	7.62	173	2.34	53	4.98	113
6	Duplicate B	17.43	1,440	43.14	2,080	3.10	147	10.95	467	7.02	307
7	None	16.00	1,400	31.71	1,600						
8	Brand C	15.14	1,360	34.14	1,600	—2.72	—173	4.33	93	0.81	—60
9	Duplicate C	8.71	1,240	38.29	1,760	—11.00	—427	10.39	347	—0.30	—40
10	None	21.57	1,800	26.00	1,320						
11	None	20.29	1,240	23.14	1,400						
12	Brand D	22.57	1,320	29.43	1,640	3.14	67	4.62	280	3.89	173
13	Duplicate D	21.86	1,520	29.71	1,680	3.29	253	3.24	360	3.26	287
14	None	17.71	1,280	28.14	1,280						

	Bus. grain.	Lbs. stover
Average increase from factory mixed fertilizers	3.94	122
Average increase from home mixed fertilizers	4.10	188

Of these factory mixtures, Brand A is one professedly manufactured especially for short season crops—potatoes and vegetables—and by an establishment for which the claim is persistently made that its tankage is acidulated as well as its Carolina rock. It would appear that our mixture of untreated tankage with acid phosphate has been quite as effective for corn as the treated factory mixture, and that its result has been effected at a very large saving in cost.

On plots 8 and 9 of Section A it will be observed that there is a decrease instead of an increase in yield from both the fertilizers. This decrease was apparently caused by planting one row of each plot too close to the deadfurrows, all the plots having been plowed into separate lands, following our uniform custom, the object being to prevent water from standing on the plot itself and to impede the crossing of the plant roots from one plot to another. It will be seen that the duplicate plots on Section B fully support the general trend of the test.

THE VALUATION OF FERTILIZERS.

Most of the fertilizer control stations give the comparative commercial values of the different brands of fertilizers which come under their inspection, in order to enable the purchaser to know whether the price asked for any special brand is a reasonable one. In arriving at these values the Stations calculate the price at which the respective constituents are being retailed for cash in the principal markets, in such standard materials as nitrate of soda, sulphate of ammonia, dried blood, tankage, bone meal, acid phosphate and muriate and sulphate of potash, and use these prices in calculating the values of mixed fertilizers.

To illustrate: Commercial nitrate of soda is found to contain on the average 15.8 per cent. of nitrogen, equivalent to 19 per cent. of "ammonia;" During 1897 nitrate of soda was retailed in eastern markets at about $44.00 per ton, which would be equivalent to 14 cents per pound for its nitrogen, and this rate was adopted by the eastern Stations in appraising the nitrate nitrogen of fertilizers. This would be equivalent to 11½ cents per pound for "ammonia."

The freight on nitrate of soda from New York to Ohio would be about $4.00 per ton in carloads, and the average retail price in Ohio may be estimated at $48.00 per ton, equivalent to 12½ cents per pound for "ammonia"—the rate used in the official valuation of the Secretary of the Ohio State Board of Agriculture.

These, it will be observed, are the prices at which nitrate of soda is sold at retail; the Ohio farmer who bought in carloads, direct of the New York importing houses, would have paid $35.00 to $38.00 per ton in New York, thus getting his ammonia in Ohio, freight paid, at 9 to 10 cents per pound.

Acid phosphate has become the chief source of fertilizer phosphoric acid. Its chief northern distributing point is Baltimore, which is as near to Ohio as to New England, and it has been sold for some time past at prices which bring the retail cost of the pound of available phosphoric acid to 5 cents in either region.

In carloads acid phophate, analyzing 14 per cent. available phosphoric acid, may be bought in Baltimore at $8.50 or less per ton, sacked, bringing the wholesale cost of the pound of available phosphoric acid to about 4¼ cents in Ohio. Sources of supply nearer home furnish the acid phosphate at about the same prices.

Muriate of potash is sold in New York at about the same price per ton as nitrate of soda, but as it is half actual potash the pound of potash costs in Ohio 4½ to 5 cents.

It has already been stated that slaughterhouse tankage is the chief source of the "ammonia" of Ohio fertilizers, nitrate of soda or sulphate of ammonia being used in extremely small quantity, if at all. While it is certainly true that the nitrogen of tankage is not so quickly available as that of nitrate of soda, yet no difference is made on this account in Ohio official valuations, the "ammonia" in a mixed fertilizer being uniformly valued at the same price as though it had been derived from nitrate of soda.

It does not follow, however, that tankage ammonia costs the price given in these valuations. For instance: The tankage used in the experiments described above is retailed in Cleveland at the uniform price of $17.00 per ton, sacked. Adding $2.00 per ton for freight its average cost to the northern Ohio farmer would be $19.00. The lot used in our work contained 5.31 per cent. nitrogen (or 6.44 per cent. ammonia) and 17.73 per cent. phosphoric acid, of which 10.31 per cent is classed as available. Valuing this available phosphoric acid at 5 cents per pound it is worth $10.31 per ton of tankage, leaving $8.69 as the cost of the 129 pounds of ammonia found in a ton, or 6¾ cents per pound.

At the present writing, tankage of this grade is quoted in Chicago at $11.50 per ton, unground in carloads. Adding $1.00 per ton for grinding and 12 cents per hundred for freight the cost in Ohio would be $14.90— say $15.00 per ton, or practically 4½ cents per pound for both the ammonia and available phosphoric acid, exclusive of sacking.

In these estimates no allowance has been made for the insoluble phosphoric acid of the tankage; but in official valuations the insoluble acid of bone and tankage is always estimated at 2 to 3 cents per pound. It is, therefore, within the limits of exact truth to say that it is possible to purchase phosphoric acid and ammonia at the same price per pound in slaughterhouse tankage.

This does not apply, however, to all grades of tankage, as those grades which run high in ammonia are more valuable to the eastern fertilizer mixers who are able to get their phosphoric acid direct from South Carolina rock much cheaper than it is sold by dealers, and to whom, therefore, the phosphoric acid of the tankage is worth much less than to the farmers of Ohio. For this reason the eastern buyers are willing to give but a nominal price for the phosphoric acid in the tankage, while the value to them of the nitrogen in the tankage is controlled by the cost of nitrogen in nitrate of soda and sulphate of ammonia, and, therefore, those grades of tankage running high in phosphoric acid and low in ammonia are relatively low priced.

CONCLUSIONS.

A little knowledge of a few of the elementary principles of chemistry is absolutely essential to the intelligent use of commercial fertilizers and such knowledge is even more important to him who buys the factory-mixed fertilizers than to him who mixes for himself.

This does not mean, however, that the farmer should become an expert analytical chemist and fit up for himself an expensive laboratory, nor that he should undertake operations which involve the chemical treatment of the materials used for fertilizing purposes.   These may be bought at first hands already treated where treatment is necessary, and in condition to use in the fertilizer drill, either separately or mixed; the farmer may buy them, in short, in just the same condition in which they are bought by the average fertilizer mixer, and he may put them together with no more elaborate machinery than a shovel on a barn floor; but in order that he may get the proper proportion of the different constituents he needs to understand enough of chemical terminology to comprehend, for example, the difference between ammonia and nitrogen, between bone phosphate and phosphoric acid, and between chemical combination and simple mixture.   He should also learn to buy on specific guaranty of composition.

By buying his fertilizers in this manner the farmer may save not only the cost of mixing, but also the margin which covers the expenses of general and traveling agents, the commissions to local dealers, the cost of carrying credit sales and insurance against bad debts—a margin which must be provided for in cash sales as well as in credit sales so long as the trade in factory-mixed fertilizers is carried on under present methods.

The experiments herein reported show, as conclusively as a single season's work can show, that there is no superiority in the factory-mixed fertilizer over the home mixture of equivalent composition, while the cost of the fertilizer is largely reduced by home mixing.